Ten Stories Up Press, First edition 2024
New York, NY

Book Cover by Molly Rosner
Illustrations by Molly Rosner

FOR ZACH AND JOEY,
WHO MADE ME A MOM AND HELP
ME FIND HUMOR AND LOVE IN
EVERY DAY.

ANXIETIES ABOUT GETTING PREGNANT

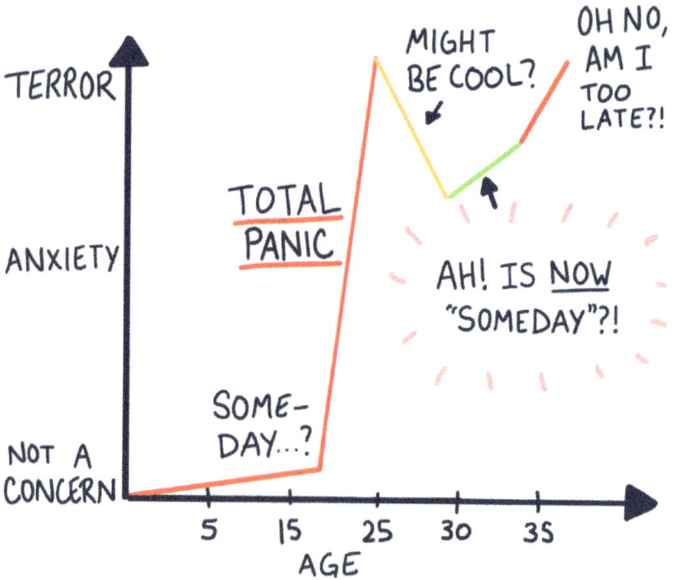

An Incomplete ⌐PREGNANCY TIMELINE

CONTENTS

Oh how motherhood changes you....

INTRODUCTION

(the only section with
a bunch of writing)

So you've peed on a stick, watched the liquid move through the tiny window, and just like that you've started your journey into motherhood! Maybe you danced and jumped, or screamed and ran to your partner, or cried, or called a friend, or stood in stunned silence while staring at a blank wall. Whatever your reaction, congratulations, you're having a baby!

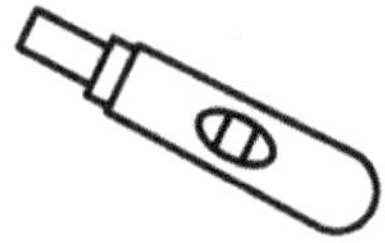

If you're like me, you feel like you have a LOT to learn, and the clock is ticking on how long you have to learn it. At 35 years old (gasp!) and having my first baby, I was a jumble of nerves and excitement.

I was so grateful to be pregnant and thrilled to become a mom (in the abstract), but when reality hit, I suddenly had a million questions.

SOME LIGHT READING

Once I told people I was pregnant, I began receiving all kinds of advice books from friends and family. Soon, I was avoiding a pile of hundreds of unread pages mocking me from the nightstand each night. The books were about pregnancy (duh), but also breastfeeding, sleep training, and relationships. I frantically downloaded no fewer than nine different pregnancy apps so I could see what size food my baby resembled each week. Between the books, the internet, and my new downloads, where would I even begin?

In my search for a sense of control, I overwhelmed myself with information I couldn't retain. How could I possibly think about sleep training and breastfeeding when I hadn't even found any pants that fit!

The one thing I found myself doing consistently throughout the 40 weeks of new changes? Drawing! Even when my belly got so big that long drawing sessions became too uncomfortable, I found condensing my experiences into single frame comics served as cathartic outlets for my confusion.

Drawing became my refuge. During virtual doula sessions amidst the uncertainty of the pandemic, it was clear that anxiety was a common thread among expecting moms. Even if our fears varied, we all had them.

PANDEMIC PREGNANT

I already felt behind and alone because I hadn't touched my Reading Pile of Shame. So I've made the book I wished I'd had - one meant solely to help share some humor and feel less alone.

Maybe this book can help you relish those moments of excitement and anticipation: Did tears come gushing out when you held that tiny pair of overalls in your hands and realized you were going to have a real, live, baby? Me too! (I then proceeded to forget where I put the overalls until my son was too big to fit into them, but that's another story.)

Pregnancy is chock full of unanticipated physical and emotional changes, relationship tests, and pushed boundaries, as well as laughs, joy, and many, many firsts. So kick your feet up (or have someone lift them on to a foot stool) and spend some time pondering your pregnancy: the things you'll miss and the things you won't; the small indignities and the pride in your belly and body as they do their thing.

Without trying to sound like an ad for Venus razors, you are a goddess in a literal sense - creating life inside of you!

But that doesn't mean you need to meet every expectation that the media and well-meaning friends lay out for you. And it definitely doesn't mean you need to shave your legs (you probably can't see them anymore anyway)!

Just remember, when this is all over, you'll have a cuddly little one who adores you whether or not you read about sleep training while they were in-utero. You can do this, even if you feel less-than-glamorous doing it.

With love,
Molly

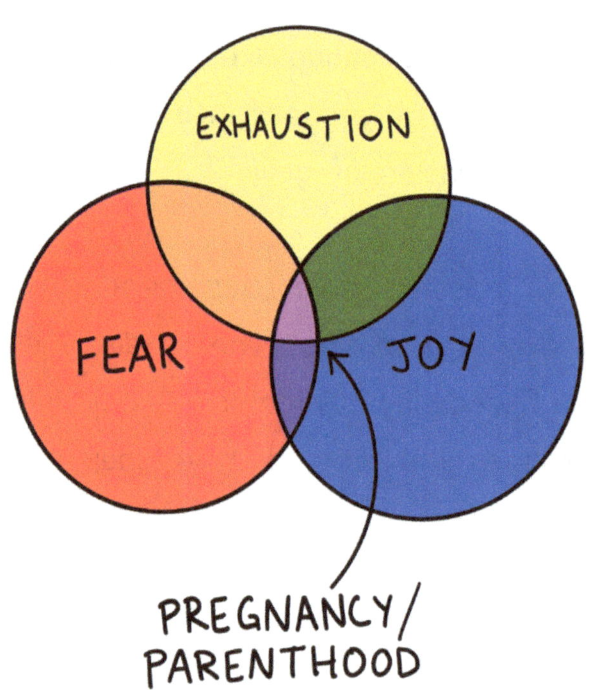

One final note - every pregnancy is different. Your first and second (and third or fourth) pregnancies will differ, too!

FIRST PREGNANCY   SECOND PREGNANCY

PRE-MOM IDENTITY
YOUR IDENTITY SHIFTS AS YOU BECOME A MOM....
YOU LEAVE SOME PARTS BEHIND...
KEEP OTHER PIECES, AND CREATE SOMETHING NEW!

WHOSE BODY IS THIS?

Being pregnant is a STRANGE adventure. Your body does weird stuff, your hormones go bananas, and you can find that you don't recognize yourself. I assure you, you are still yourself, but you're also going through a major transformation. Incredible!

Once you have your baby, lots of people talk about how things change but things started changing for you as soon as that sperm hit the egg(s) - and in unpredictable ways.

I DON'T KNOW WHY I FEEL SO SICK
KAPOW!
BAM!

Say goodbye to those toes. Even swollen feet

won't be competition for the belly swell.

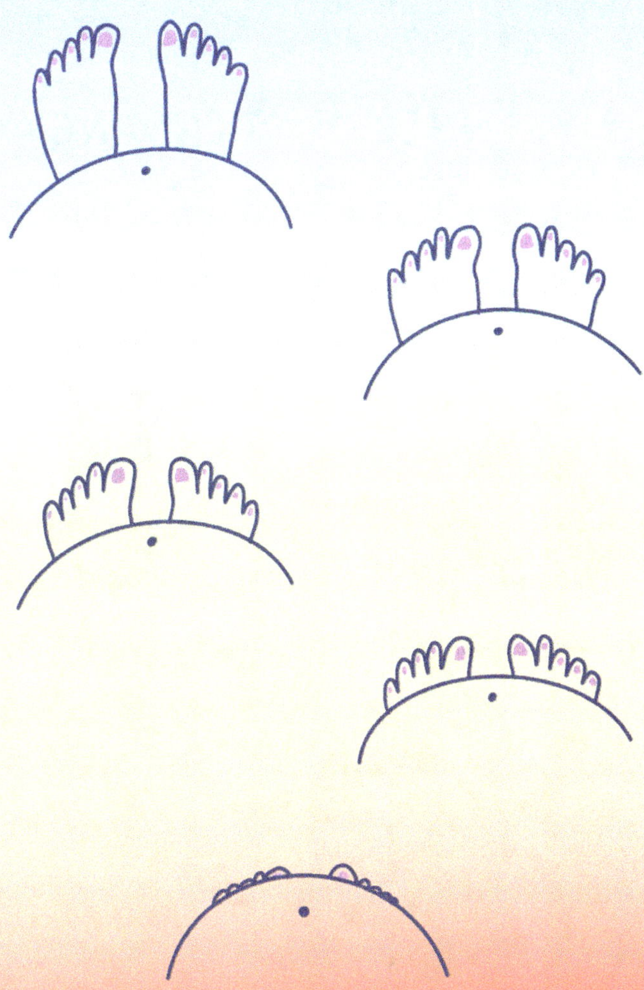

FOOT SUNSET

MYSTERIES OF PREGNANCY

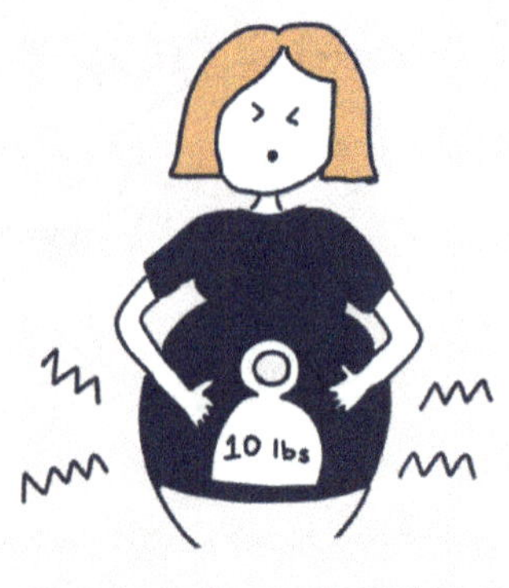

CONSTIPATED?

STOMACH BUG?

OH RIGHT... PREGNANT!

If it's your second child, buckle up - the
kicks get doubled!

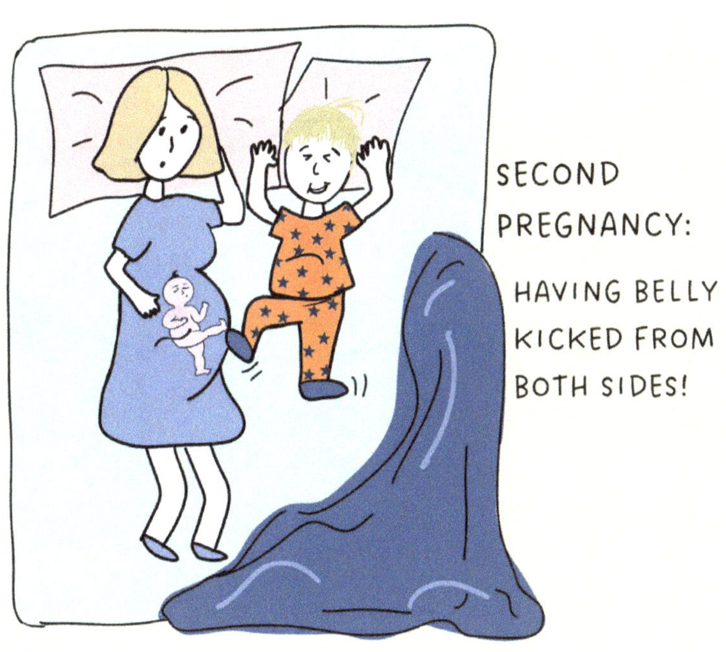

I LOOK LIKE A HOUSE...
I FEEL LIKE A HOUSE...

WAIT, I AM SOMEONE'S HOUSE!

FASHIONISTA

ZIP!
3 MONTHS
PREGNANT
5 MONTHS...
ZZIP...

7 MONTHS
PREGNANT

DEEP
INHALE
ZIIIIIP...

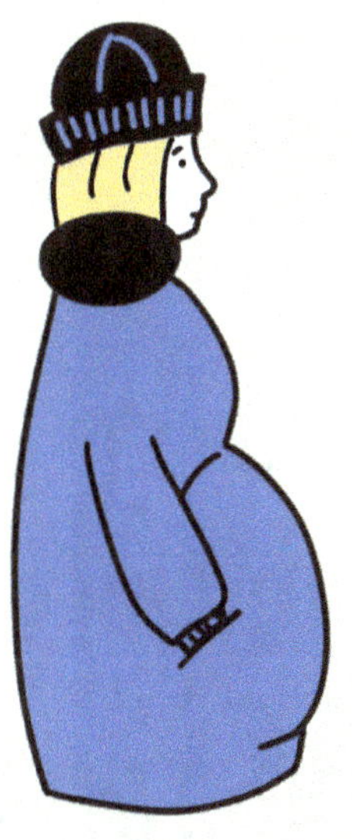

WILL SPRING
ARRIVE BEFORE I
CAN'T FIT IN MY
COAT?

I'VE NEVER
OWNED A CROP TOP
BEFORE...

NOW I
EXCLUSIVELY
OWN CROP TOPS

WHICH DRESS GOES BEST WITH GREEN?

MY CUPS RUNNETH OVER

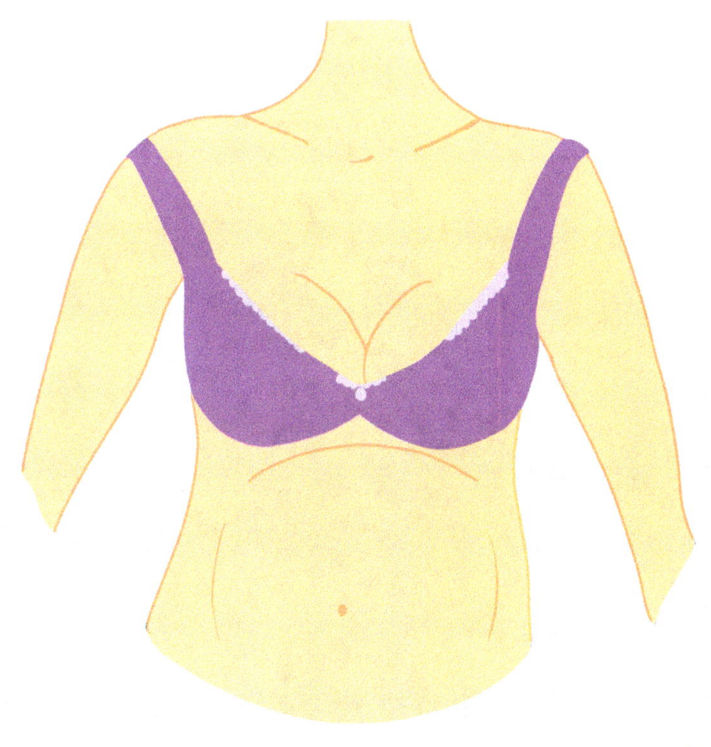

PREGNANT FASHIONISTA

OPTION 1

RESEMBLE A HOUSE
IN A MAXI DRESS

OPTION 2

SHOW OFF THOSE UNSHAVEN LEGS
THAT YOU CAN'T REACH

NO, I'M NOT EVEN TRYING PANTS.

UNSOLICITED ADVICE

Beware that you may internalize all the expectations and guilt that outside influences foist onto new and expecting moms. Fatigue is REAL. You're not being lazy. Don't let external expectations cloud your experience of pregnancy.

I SHOULD BE DOING MORE...

A MOTHER'S GUILT STARTS EARLY

Once you find out you're pregnant - and just as you're at your most vulnerable - you can look forward to months, nay a lifetime, of unsolicited advice from your closest relatives or random strangers on the street. And don't worry - a lot of it will be conflicting advice!

You are not required to find pregnancy magical. Nor does parenthood mean giving up everything you once loved. Give yourself some grace by ignoring the most common cliched things people say to you...

PREGNANCY CLICHE BINGO

GIVE YOURSELF A LITTLE TREAT EACH TIME YOU GET 3 CLICHES!

SLEEP WHEN THE BABY SLEEPS	YOU'RE TIRED NOW? JUST YOU WAIT!	YOU SURE IT'S NOT TWINS?
WHY WON'T YOU TELL ME THE SEX?	YOU'RE ABOUT TO POP!	WILL YOU HAVE ANOTHER?
DON'T DO THAT!	DON'T EAT THAT!	DON'T DRINK THAT!

Take every label you're given with
a grain of salt...

WHAT I
PICTURE
WHEN
THEY SAY...

GERIATRIC PREGNANCY

You never know what challenges pregnancy (and parenthood) will bring. Your biggest challenge may not be what you expect. I still have PTSD from phone calls with my insurance company.

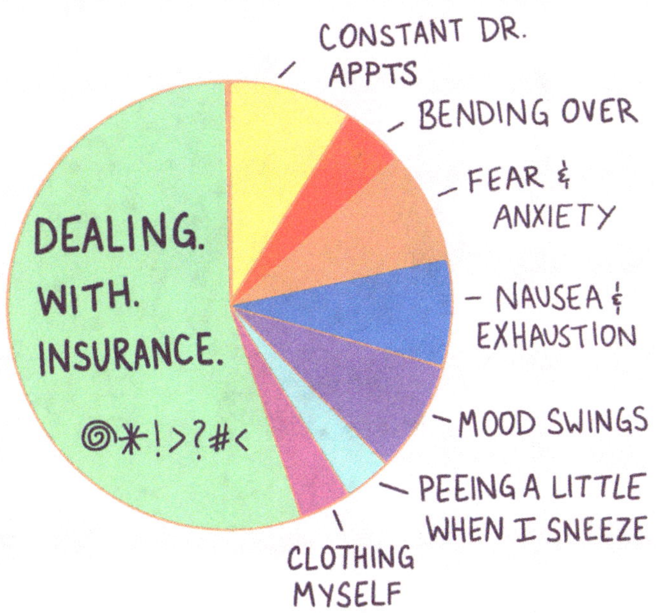

Remember, context matters!

EXCEPT
IN
NYC
YOU'RE
HAVING KIDS
ALREADY?

PARTNERSHIPS

You're going to have to prioritize your comfort, health, and yourself during this time. It may take a little bit of explaining to your partner...

ALL. THE. PILLOWS.

and your partner may have to put your
mind at ease sometimes....

WEIRD NEW RITUALS

WHEN I'M FEELING GOOD...

OUR BABY IS SO WIGGLY TODAY!
FATHER OF MY CHILD

WHEN I'M FEELING BAD...

YOUR CHILD IS KICKING ME.

This is an argument you may continue to
have for the next 18 years...

With pregnancy, your needs and abilities shift...

THIRD TRIMESTER

Whether you feel like it or not, you're already a mom. You might not play music for your fetus or have a fully decorated nursery ready to go, but you wonder about your child, you keep yourself going, and that in turn keeps your child growing, nurtured by you!

?!?!
DUE DATE
9 MONTHS
8 MONTHS
7 MONTHS
<PANT>
HELLO... THIRD...
<PANT>
TRIMESTER

PREGNANCY OLYMPICS

SHOT-PUTTING ON SHOES
MARATHON BLADDER CONTROL
PARK WADDLING
EXTREME FLOOR SITTING
WORRY NAPPING

DON'T MIND ME... JUST GROWING A
WHOLE HUMAN ON SWOLLEN FEET
AFTER A LONG DAY AT WORK.

8 MONTHS IN AND I STILL GET SURPRISED BY MY OWN REFLECTION

You may find yourself doing weird
nonsensical things...

ALTERING LYRICS FOR BABY'S ABILITIES

WHAT ARE YOU DOING?

SEEING IF THE BABY'S KICKS SAY "HAPPY MOTHER'S DAY" IN MORSE CODE

In your third trimester, you may fully lose control of your emotions. Remember, your hormones are going bonkers and they will continue to do so into your fourth trimester. Maybe it's your first lesson in letting go of control as a parent.

THINGS THAT MADE ME CRY IN MY THIRD TRIMESTER...

HOLDING A TINY PAIR OF OVERALLS

HEARING ANY LOVE SONG AND THINKING IT'S ABOUT MY BABY

A BEAUTIFUL TREE IN THE PARK

WHEN MY HUSBAND DIDN'T
BRING ME WATER

AND ALSO... 

WHEN MY HUSBAND DID
BRING ME WATER

A SUMMER
THIRD TRIMESTER

EXPECTATION FOR MY PREGNANT SUMMER

REALITY

REALITY

REALITY

REGULAR NAP TIME
(DUE TO INSOMNIA)

REALITY

SEE YOU NEXT WEEK, DOC!
DON'T FORGET TO PEE IN A CUP BEFORE YOU LEAVE!
EXAM ROOM 3

WHAT CAN'T THIS BELLY DO?

BOOKSHELF

TABLE

CRUMB CATCHER

SCI-FI SPECIAL EFFECTS

WORKING FROM HOME

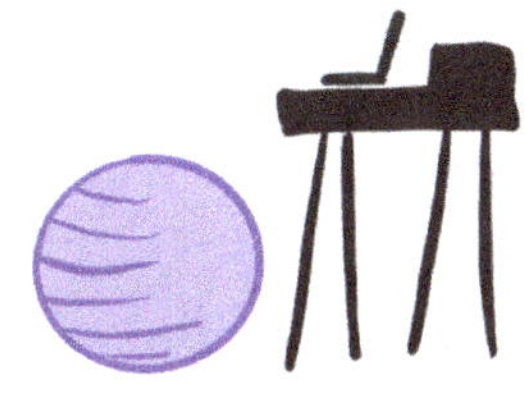

YOGA BALL AT DESK

LAPTOP IN BED

LYING ON SIDE IN BED

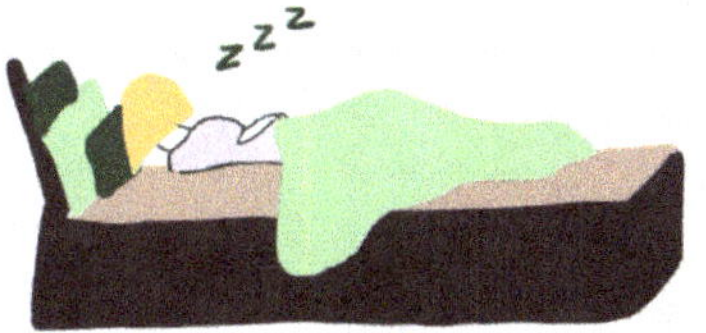

ASLEEP

HORMONES HAVE TAKEN CONTROL,

STEP AWAY FROM THE SPONGE...

NESTING, WHEN YOU'RE 38 WEEKS PREGNANT AND YOU CAN'T REALLY DO ANYTHING!

THE SIREN SOUND OF THAT
BEAUTIFUL TRUCK

MOVE OVER, KIDS!
(I'M GONNA BE A GREAT MOM..)

PRENATAL YOGA

You've walked 10,000 steps today!
HOW? I HAVEN'T LEFT THE HOUSE?

THIRD TRIMESTER
MEANS CHECKING
THE WEATHER
FROM MY PHONE...

WEATHER

...BECAUSE THE
WINDOW IS TOO
FAR AWAY

THIRD TRIMESTER MATH

GOOGLE SAYS IT'S AN 8 MINUTE WALK SO...

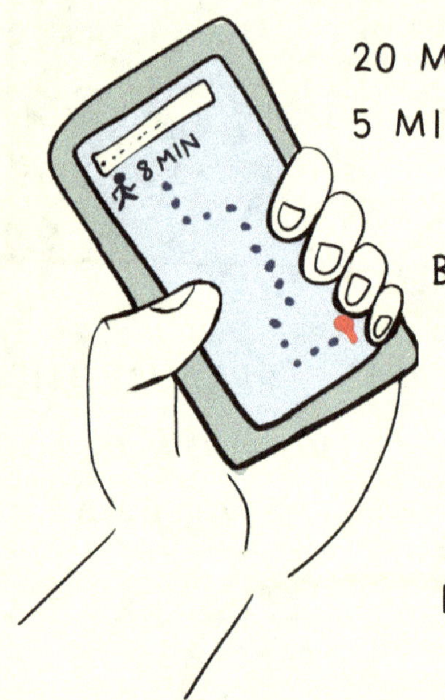

20 MINUTE WALK + 5 MINUTES OF REST. CAN'T WALK BACK OR CARRY A LOT, SO $15 UBER RIDE HOME SINCE THE SUBWAY HAS TOO MANY STAIRS...

FORGET IT, I'LL JUST STAY HOME.

SUDDENLY AN EXISTENTIAL QUESTION

THERE ARE BOOKS WITH WAIT TIMES FURTHER AWAY THAN MY DUE DATE...

DO I EVEN BOTHER?

BABY IS HERE!

CONCLUDING THOUGHTS...

While a lot of your time may not feel like your own anymore, you'll be amazed by how much you can get done in the small pockets of time you get as a mom. Even if that just means taking a nap, that's a victory and will recharge you for all the other things you'll accomplish.

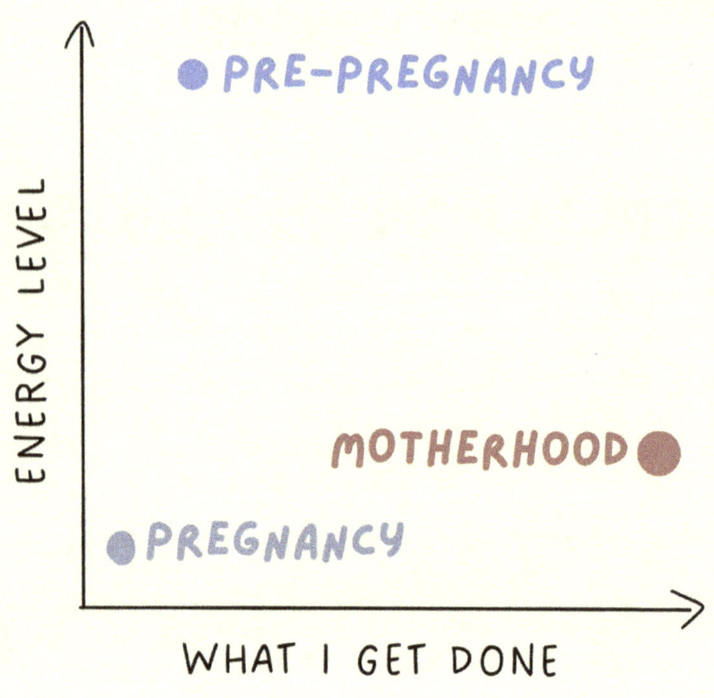

Give yourself grace during those early months. The fourth trimester is no joke and you will need to carve out boundaries that feel best for you.

WE INTERRUPT OUR REGULARLY SCHEDULED PROGRAMMING...

If you're anxious, like me, happiness might always seem fragile. You may feel as though the slightest misstep will break the delicate bit of joy you've built around you.

Parenthood expands the joy you feel so much but with it expands anxiety, fear, and that feeling of fragility.

POST-BABY

YOUR HEART SUDDENLY EXISTS
OUTSIDE OF YOU

JOYS AND TRIUMPHS FEEL HUGE,
BUT ALSO FRAGILE

A lot of people might say, "you've got this!" and that's true! But your level of confidence will continue to surge and wane from now until... well, I haven't figured out when that will end yet.

CONFIDENCE IN MOTHERING ABILITIES

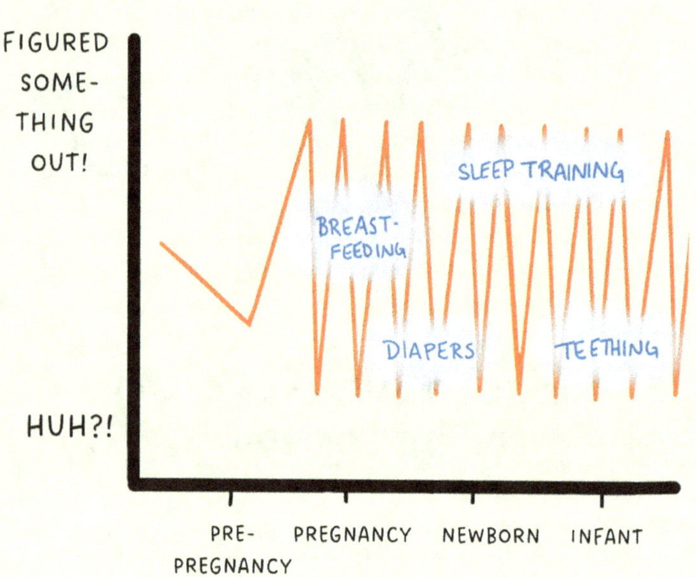

WISHING YOU
CALM AND JOY AS YOU
MOVE TOWARDS MOTHERHOOD

- What physical & emotional symptoms surprised you during your pregnancy?
- What has been most challenging/fun as you experiment with your clothing?
- What has been the best advice you've received?
- What has been the worst advice you've received?
- What surprising, unsolicited thoughts have you been given?
- Who has had opinions about your pregnancy that you wouldn't have expected?
- What has been most challenging or surprising about your relationship during pregnancy?
- How is your partner preparing for the baby?
- What emotions do you feel when you imagine meeting your baby?
- What do you think will be best or most challenging about postpartum life?
- What have you been most grateful for?
- How did you choose a name for your baby?
- What do you hope to remember about your pregnancy / tell your child about?

I LEAVE YOU WITH A FEW AFFIRMATIONS TO
HANG ON TO DURING THIS TRANSITION:

Taking care of myself IS taking care of my
family.

I am brave enough to ask for help
when I need it.

I will listen to my body
and trust what it tells me.

I am strong and capable of loving deeply.

I'm going to be an amazing mom!

ADD YOUR OWN HERE:

____

____

____

____

LET'S KEEP IN TOUCH!

To hear about new projects & resources for new and expecting moms, including the follow up to this book about motherhood, join my mailing list over at: www.mobotdoodles.com

If you enjoyed this book, please consider leaving a review of this book on Goodreads or Storygraph. Reviews help other people who may enjoy this book find it! To keep hearing about projects like this one, you can scan the QR code below with your phone's camera:

THANK YOU!!

ACKNOWLEDGMENTS

At its core, this book is about love amidst transformation. I am so grateful to everyone who has supported this project as I began the adventure of motherhood. Thanks to my family: Paul, Zach, Joey, Eva, "Big Zach," Emilie, Owen, Margot, and of course, my mom and dad. To the friends who served as early readers, thank you for your thoughtful feedback: Max, Sarah, Miriam, Katie, Anna, Rachel, and Jackie. I am so lucky to have heard input from these incredible friends/moms. Thank you to Caitlin, Julie & Smiley for the invaluable advice on getting this book into the world. Thank you Petrushka, Kathleen, and "The Moms Group" who have gotten me through my second time postpartum while I completed this project. Thank you Emelie for believing in this project enough to take me on as a client and Karolina for your work on formatting.

And thank you to everyone who showed even the smallest bit of interest in this dream of mine. I am filled with deep gratitude.

Molly Rosner is a mom of what feels like 1,000 kids living in New York City, where she was born and raised. She holds an MA and PhD and works as an educator at universities and museums around the city.

She likes to draw and write about the things she loves: NYC and life with her family. She is the author of the book "Playing With History: American Identities and Children's Consumer Culture."

Her artwork has been called "rudimentary" and "low-brow"!

SEE YOU

ON THE

OTHER SIDE!

www.ingramcontent.com/pod-product-compliance
Lightning Source LLC
Chambersburg PA
CBHW070614170726
48004CB00018B/1354